SIMPLY SCIENCE

Satellites
and the GPS

by Natalie M. Rosinsky

Content Adviser: Mats Selen, Ph.D.,
Department of Physics, University of Illinois at Champaign-Urbana

Science Adviser: Terrence E. Young Jr., M.Ed., M.L.S.,
Jefferson Parish (La.) Public Schools

Reading Adviser: Dr. Linda D. Labbo,
Department of Reading Education, College of Education,
The University of Georgia

COMPASS POINT BOOKS
MINNEAPOLIS, MINNESOTA

Compass Point Books
3109 West 50th Street, #115
Minneapolis, MN 55410

Visit Compass Point Books on the Internet at *www.compasspointbooks.com*
or e-mail your request to *custserv@compasspointbooks.com*

Photographs ©: The Boeing Company, cover; DigitalVision, 4, 5, 7; Reuters NewMedia Inc./Corbis, 8, 27, 28; Bettmann/Corbis, 10; NASA, 11, 26; Courtesy of NASA/JPL/Caltech, 12; PhotoDisc, 13, 14; USDA/ARS/Jack Dykinga, 15; Leif Skoogfors/Corbis, 16; Aerospace Corp./Tom Stack & Associates, 18; Index Stock Imagery/Carol Werner, 19; AFP/Corbis, 20; Rockwell/TSADO/Tom Stack & Associates, 22; Therisa Stack/Tom Stack & Associates, 23; Comstock, 24; James Leynse/ Corbis SABA, 29; John Cross/The Free Press, 32.

Editor: Catherine Neitge
Photo Researcher: Svetlana Zhurkina
Designer/Page Production: Bradfordesign, Inc./The Design Lab

Library of Congress Cataloging-in-Publication Data
Rosinsky, Natalie M. (Natalie Myra)
    Satellites and the GPS / by Natalie Rosinsky.
        p. cm. — (Simply science)
Includes index.
Summary: A brief introduction to the history, characteristics, and importance of satellites, especially those that make up the Global Positioning System.
    ISBN 0-7565-0597-6 (hardcover)
1. Global Positioning System—Juvenile literature. 2. Artificial satellites in navigation—Juvenile literature. [1. Artificial satellites. 2. Global Positioning System.] I. Title. II. Series: Simply science (Minneapolis, Minn.)
    TL798.N3R67 2004
    910'.285—dc22   2003014413

Table of Contents

*Note: In this book, words that are defined in the glossary are in **bold** the first time they appear in the text.*

Circling High Above Earth

There are important machines in the sky! These machines called satellites circle Earth in **orbits.** Their orbits are so high that you may never see one. Most satellites travel between about 300 and 23,000 miles (483 and 37,007 kilometers) above Earth. This is above Earth's **atmosphere,** out in space.

Satellites must travel very fast to stay in

Nearly 2,500 satellites orbit Earth. Different companies and countries own them.

A satellite speeds along high above the clouds.

orbit. The highest satellites speed along at 7,000 miles (11,263 km) per hour. Lower flying satellites race along at more than 17,000 miles (27,353 km) per hour!

All satellites need a power source. Most satellites get power from the sun. Their **solar panels** gather energy from the sun and change it into electricity. Satellites carry instruments that do different jobs. Satellites contact people on Earth about these jobs through radio waves. People also use radio waves to send messages to satellites.

A satellite's solar panels collect energy from the sun.

Satellites Then and Now

In 1957, Russia sent the very first satellite into space. *Sputnik 1* was the size of a basketball. It weighed less than 200 pounds (91 kilograms). In 1958, the United States sent its own satellite into space. It was called *Explorer 1*. Many other satellites followed. All these satellites were **launched** into space with rockets. Each blastoff had bursts of fire and loud roars!

By 1971, the United States was sending much bigger satellites into space. A few were made to carry people. Three **astronauts** were able

A replica of Sputnik 1 hangs from the ceiling at the Smithsonian's Air and Space Museum in Washington, D.C.

to live and work aboard a space station called *Skylab*. Other space stations have been sent into space and orbited Earth since then.

In 1981, a new "space age" began for some satellites. The space shuttle *Columbia* put a satellite into orbit. In the 1980s, more satellites were launched using the space shuttle. Most satellites, though, are still launched into space with rockets. Sometimes the satellites have

Astronauts at the Kennedy Space Center get ready for takeoff to the Skylab space station in 1973.

Astronauts perch on a space shuttle robotic arm ▶ to repair the Hubble Space Telescope in 1993.

to be repaired in space by the shuttle crew. The orbiting Hubble Space Telescope was fixed this way. It is a large telescope in space.

Many Kinds of Satellites

A few satellites are sent on long trips to other worlds. The spacecraft *Galileo* carried many instruments. It orbited Jupiter and told scientists much about the planet. Most satellites, though, orbit Earth. They do jobs that help people every day.

Some satellites help people keep in touch. Phone and TV signals may use satellites. Signals from one area on Earth are sent to a

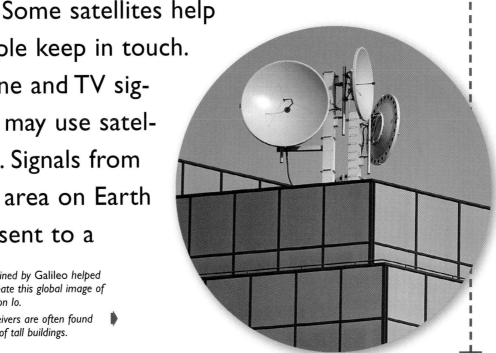

Images obtained by Galileo helped scientists create this global image of Jupiter's moon Io.

Satellite receivers are often found on the tops of tall buildings.

communications satellite. This machine then relays messages to a receiver in another area on Earth. You may have seen TV receivers. They look like big dishes. When you watch TV, you may be using a satellite!

Some satellites fly low above Earth. They keep track of the weather. Often, weather reports have information and pictures taken by these satellites.

Other satellites provide images that help farmers keep track of growing

A satellite image shows a hurricane swirling toward the Southern United States.

Scientists adjust a radar dish (left) and get ready to launch a weather balloon that will be tracked by a satellite. They are studying the effects of winds.

crops. Different satellites help scientists learn more about Earth and its oceans. There are spy satellites, too! These satellites locate and track things and people.

Where Is Everyone?

Today, there is an important group of satellites called the Global Positioning System (GPS). It locates people and things all around the world. This group began as a military tool. In 1978, the United States Navy started launching GPS satellites.

The Global Positioning System helped American soldiers in the Gulf War. After that, the government built up the system further. Today, the GPS is still managed by the Department of Defense. It is widely used by nonmilitary people, too.

◀ *Soldiers use a GPS receiver to map an area.*

There are three parts to the Global Positioning System. There are the satellites themselves. Then there are the machinery and people controlling the satellites. Finally, there are the small computers called receivers. These receivers give GPS users information about their position on Earth.

At least 24 satellites orbit Earth as part of the Global Positioning System. Each one weighs 2,000 pounds (908 kg),

There are at least 24 GPS satellites operating at all times.

A GPS satellite orbits Earth.

is 17 feet (5 meters) across, and lasts up to 10 years. They speed along at about 8,700 miles (13,998 km) per

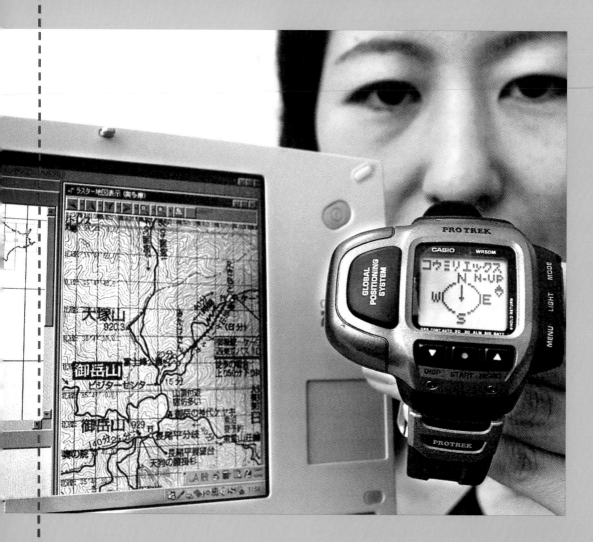

hour at **altitudes** of about 12,000 miles (19,308 km). Five ground stations track and control the satellites. Four tracking stations are on islands around the world. The control station and another tracking station are in Colorado. There are ground antennas all over the world, too.

The first GPS receivers were the size and shape of backpacks. Today, most receivers are the size of cell phones. There is even a GPS receiver small enough to fit into a wristwatch! More than 100 different models of GPS receivers are for sale.

◀ A Japanese GPS receiver is small enough to fit into a wristwatch.

How the Global Positioning System Works

Each GPS satellite carries a special clock. These clocks make sure GPS satellites send signals at exactly the same time.

The satellites send many regular signals. A GPS receiver combines signals from the four GPS satellites nearest it. The receiver also has the location of these

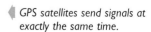

GPS satellites send signals at exactly the same time.

A receiver shows exact location.

satellites. Its computer combines all
this information and uses it to figure
out its own location. This **waypoint** is

then shown on the receiver to the person using it. The receiver stores information about many waypoints. It can also show how far a user must travel to reach someplace. It can show how long this trip will take.

Information is sent among control stations, satellites, and receivers by radio waves. These radio waves do not pass through solid objects. This is why the GPS only works outdoors. It cannot be used underground. Sometimes, it will not work near mountains or tall buildings. Even forests with big, leafy trees sometimes cause problems for GPS receivers!

Because it uses radio waves, the GPS sometimes will not work near mountains.

Ways the Global Positioning System Helps

The GPS helps keep many people safe. Ships and airplanes use it to **navigate** in bad weather. Police and firefighters use it to reach people in danger quickly. Campers and scientists in wild areas use it, too. GPS keeps them from getting lost in places without street signs or familiar **landmarks**. Today, most GPS

A GPS receiver and a round camera mounted on a helicopter help firefighters locate brush fires in Florida.

An elephant in Kenya wears a GPS receiver around its neck.

receivers show position correctly within 10 to 20 feet (3 to 6 m).

Other people use the GPS at work. Scientists use it to locate minerals and keep track of animals that wear special

collars. Farmers use it to keep track of crops. Companies use the GPS to find shorter ways to send packages. Mapmakers use it to make maps kept in computers.

For some people, the GPS is a fun "extra." Some new cars now come with GPS receivers. Their drivers will not get lost!

The GPS is one way that satellites have become part of our everyday lives.

A dog in Japan wears a new, very small GPS receiver that allows its owners to keep track of their pet.

A car features a GPS receiver in the dashboard.

Glossary

altitude—the height of something above the ground

astronauts—people who travel into outer space

atmosphere—the layer of gases around a planet

landmarks—objects that help people recognize their location

launched—put into motion

navigate—to find the way to someplace

orbit—the path through space that something follows as it moves around a planet or other heavenly body

solar panels—a system that turns sunlight into electricity to power equipment

waypoint—a position shown on a GPS receiver

Did You Know?

- More than 20 countries have sent satellites into orbit around Earth.

- Solar-powered satellites use little electricity. Many satellites use no more electricity than an electric toaster!

Want to Know More?

At the Library

Barrett, N. S. *The Picture World of Rockets and Satellites*. New York: Franklin Watts, 1990.

Berger, Melvin, and Gilda Berger. *Can You Hear a Shout in Space? Questions and Answers About Space Exploration*. New York: Scholastic, 2000.

Stille, Darlene R. *Satellites*. Minneapolis: Compass Point Books, 2002.

Walker, Niki. *Satellites and Space Probes*. New York: Crabtree Publishing, 1998.

On the Web

For more information on *satellites and the GPS,* use FactHound to track down Web sites related to this book.

1. Go to *www.compasspointbooks.com/facthound*
2. Type in this book ID: 0756505976
3. Click on the *Fetch It* button.

Your trusty FactHound will fetch the best Web sites for you!

Through the Mail

National Aeronautics and Space Administration (NASA)

Headquarters Information Center

300 E St. S.W.

Washington, DC 20560

education@nasa.gov

To ask for free brochures, stickers, and other information about the space program

On the Road

Kennedy Space Center

Cape Canaveral, FL 32899

321/452-2121

To walk through a full-size space shuttle and learn more about the space program

Index

About the Author

Natalie M. Rosinsky writes about science, economics, history, and other fun things. One of her two cats usually sits on her computer as she works in Mankato, Minnesota. Natalie earned graduate degrees from the University of Wisconsin and has been a high school and college teacher.